The Social Work Pocket Guide to… Stress and Burnout
By Siobhan Maclean

First Edition 2011 ISBN: 978-1-903575-72-7

A catalogue record for this book will be available from t

©Kirwin Maclean Associates Ltd 4 Mesnes Green, Lichfield, Staffs, WS

Printed in Great Britain by 4edge Limited.

Contents List...

What?

Why?

How?

WHAT?

People often talk about stress, but if you ask someone what stress is they might struggle to explain it. We all feel that we know what stress is and we all feel that we have experienced it, but it can mean quite different things to different people. There are also different models of stress, which influence the various definitions of stress.

This pocket guide therefore begins by exploring the following questions:

- What is stress?

- What are the main models of stress?

- What is work-related stress?

- What is burnout?

- What is compassion fatigue?

- What is Post-Traumatic Stress?

- What causes stress?

- What are the signs and symptoms of stress?

WHAT IS STRESS ALL ABOUT?

Stress is:

The body's reaction to a change that requires a physical, mental or emotional adjustment or response.

(Morrow 2010)

The adverse reaction a person has to excessive pressure or other types of demand placed upon them.

(Health and Safety Executive 2007)

A Family of related experiences, pathways, responses and outcomes caused by a range of different events or circumstances. Different people experience different aspects.

(Mind Tools 2010)

What?

A reaction which occurs when an individual perceives that the demands of an external situation are beyond his or her perceived ability to cope with them.

(Lazarus 1966)

....perceived in the mind, suffered in the human spirit, experienced via the emotions, expressed in behaviour, and 'held' in the body.

(Anon quoted by ISMA 2009)

Systemic Model of Stress

The word stress was first coined in the 1930s by an endocrinologist Hans Selye. In the 1920s Walter Cannon had recognised the instinctive 'fight or flight' response. When a person experiences shock or anticipates a threat, it quickly releases hormones which help it to survive. These hormones help a person to run faster or fight harder. Selye built upon this to develop a model of stress which is still widely used today.

Understanding stress in a biological sense helps us to see that stress is a natural reaction – it is what helps us to get up in the morning and what helps us to function. In itself, stress is not a bad thing. Too little stress is certainly not a good thing – it means the body is under stimulated leaving a person bored. This can lead people to seeking out "thrills" to create some stress.

What?

Selye (e.g.: 1975) developed a number of terms when exploring stress. In trying to understand the systemic model it can be useful to understand his thoughts:

Stress is a reaction

Eustress is a term which can be used to describe when stress enhances functioning

Distress is persistent stress which goes unresolved and can lead to anxiety or depression

A **Stressor** is a stimulus causing the reaction

Forms of Stress

Acute Stress

This describes short term experiences of extreme stress. Small doses of stress can be thrilling and exhilarating. Some people seek out small amounts or short 'doses' of stress for the 'thrill of it'. Too much stress through can cause psychological distress and negative physical symptoms.

"SHORT TERM STRESS CAN BE A THRILL"

Chronic stress

This describes long term stress that grinds people down. Whilst people are well aware of acute stress, people can get used to chronic stress. They might miss the symptoms in the drama or crisis of the situation causing the stress. People can learn to live with chronic stress which actually makes it more dangerous.

What?

Psychological Model of stress

This model, also referred to as the transactional model of stress, was first developed by Lazarus in 1966. This model views stress not as an automatic physical response but as a relationship between a person and their environment. Stress is viewed as a 'transaction' or a balance. People are seen as facing stress when there is an imbalance between the demands placed on them and the resources they have to deal with those demands.

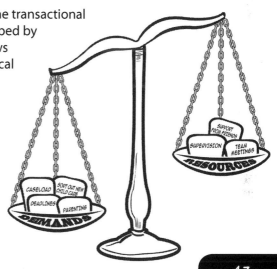

Work-related stress is:

..experienced when the demands of the work environment exceed the worker's ability to cope with them.

(Milczarek, Schneider and Gonzalez 2009: 14)

...one of the biggest health and safety challenges that we face in Europe. Nearly one in four workers is affected by it, and studies suggest that between 50% and 60% of all lost working days are related to it.

(European Agency for Safety and Health at Work 2010)

What?

Facts and figures

Research (Milczarek, Schneider and Gonzalez 2009 and Health and Safety Executive 2007) indicates:

- Stress is the second most work-related health problem affecting 22% of workers. Only musculoskeletal problems are more likely to damage health.

- Work-related stress is most likely to affect people aged between 45 and 54.

- The highest levels of stress are reported by professionals and associate professionals.

- 10 million working days are lost in the UK each year because of work-related stress.

- Work-related stress cost the UK more than £530 million in 2005/2006.

Burnout is:

A syndrome of emotional exhaustion and cynicism that occurs frequently among individuals who do 'people-work' of some kind.

(Maslach and Jackson 1981: 99)

When our minds and bodies simply cannot continue to function. It can lead to serious emotional or physical illness.

(McKinnon 1998: 1)

The dislocation between what people are and what they have to do. It represents an erosion in values, dignity, spirit and will – an erosion of the human soul. It is a malady that spreads gradually and continuously over time, putting people into a downward spiral from which it's hard to recover….

(Maslach and Leiter 1997: 17)

What?

What are the differences between stress and burnout?

Stress	Burnout
Characterised by over-engagement	Characterised by disengagement
Emotions become over-active	Emotions become blunted
Primary damage is physical	Primary damage is emotional
Exhaustion affects physical energy	Exhaustion affects motivation and drive
Loss of fuel and energy	Loss of ideals and hope
Produces a sense of urgency and hyperactivity	Produces a sense of helplessness and hopelessness
Feelings of panic, phobias and anxiety type disorders	Feelings of paranoia, depersonalisation and detachment

(Adapted from Croucher 2010)

Compassion fatigue is:

A deep physical, emotional and spiritual exhaustion accompanied by acute emotional pain.
Those who have experienced compassion fatigue describe it as being sucked into a vortex that pulls them slowly downward. They have no idea how to stop the downward spiral so they work harder and continue to give to others until they are completely tapped out.

(Pfifferling and Gilley 2000)

Symptomized by the normal displays of chronic stress. It results from the care giving work caregivers chose to do. Day in, day out workers struggle to function in care giving environments that constantly present heart wrenching emotional challenges. Eventually negative attitudes prevail.

(Compassion Fatigue Awareness Project 2010)

What?

Many of the social workers I meet on a daily basis talk about losing the passion they once had for social work. Gradually (sometimes very slowly) the "light" fades. Maybe the light dims as the pressures of change and the negativity about social work covers it. To me, this is the beginning of compassion fatigue. There is a sense of 'doing the job' but feeling very negative about it – being sucked into that 'downward spiral' and allowing the light to fade. The most important thing that supports social workers in this position is rediscovering their passion for social work.

Social work practice educators often talk about the "lightbulb moment" with student social workers – when we see the lightbulb go on. I am often left feeling concerned though about how long the bulb keeps glowing (will it burn out?)

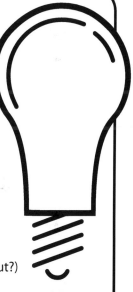

Post-Traumatic Stress is:

A trauma is a wound. Post-Traumatic Stress Disorder refers to deep emotional wounds. In 1980 following the Vietnam experience, the American Psychiatric Association formally defined Post Traumatic Stress Disorder categorising it as one of the anxiety disorders.

(Schiraldi 2009)

Post-Traumatic Stress can arise after a person has been exposed to a traumatic event. A traumatic event is something in which the person is exposed to actual or threatened harm. Post-Traumatic Stress Disorder is diagnosed when the person who has experienced the traumatic event experiences for a month or more a range of defined symptoms.

(Taylor 2006: 170)

What?

Secondary-Traumatic Stress is:

...also referred to as vicarious trauma. It occurs when a stressful situation doesn't happen to you directly but you feel its effects through listening to the person who has experienced the traumatic event. You are more prone to experiencing secondary trauma if your life is 'out of balance'.

(McKenna 2006)

...the natural consequent behaviours resulting from knowledge about a traumatising event experienced by a significant other. It is the stress resulting from wanting to help a traumatised or suffering person.

(Figley 1995)

What are the signs and symptoms of stress?

As individuals everyone will react to stress in different ways. However, people generally react to stress in three dimensions – physical (sometimes referred to as physiological), emotional (psychological) and behavioural.

Behavioural responses are based on significant changes in a person's behaviour.

Physiological responses are based on a stimulation of the autonomic nervous system, and changes in bodily systems.

Psychological responses include strong negative emotions, anger, anxiety, irritation, depression etc. These are accompanied by changes in cognition including decreased self-esteem.

This means that the signs and symptoms of stress are generally seen in the three dimensions.

What?

Physical reactions to stress

Someone experiencing stress might experience:

Muscle tension	Tiredness	Indigestion
Aches and pains	Headaches	Hair loss
Sweating	Frequency in urinating	Chest pain
Twitches	Dilated pupils	Butterflies in the stomach
Pins and needles	Rapid or uneven heartbeat	Rapid breathing
Nausea	Sleep disturbance	Constipation or diarrhoea
Dry mouth	Restlessness and fidgeting	Lack of concentration

Emotional reactions to stress

Someone who is experiencing stress may have exaggerated emotional reactions. They may feel:

Tense	Irritable	Agitated
Under pressure	Tearful	Suspicious
Mentally drained	Unable to relax	Restless
Fear	Conflict	Indecisive
Frustration	Gloomy	Negative
Anger	Embarrassed	

What?

Behavioural reactions to stress

Someone experiencing stress might:

- Sleep much less than usual or much more than usual
- Become withdrawn where they were once very sociable
- Become irritable and snap at people
- Engage in behaviours to constantly seek reassurance
- Smoke more
- Make more mistakes
- Become dependent on drink or drugs
- Engage in self harming behaviours
- Change their sexual behaviours (loss of interest, increase in casual sex)
- Engage in obsessive type behaviours (e.g.: excessively checking things are switched off)

25

What causes stress?

Although it is clear that different people find different things stressful, it is generally accepted that some life events are more stressful than others:

Stress rating: Very High	Stress rating: High	Stress rating: Moderate
Death of a partner or close family member	Marital reconciliation	Family arguments
Divorce or separation	Retirement	Legal action over debt
Jail term	Serious illness of a family member	Change in responsibilities at work
Personal injury or illness	Pregnancy	Son or daughter leaving home
Loss of job	Difficulties in intimacy	Conflict at work
Moving house	Change of job	
	Financial problems	
	Death of a close friend	

(adapted from Wilkinson 2003)

What?

Essentially the causes of stress can be categorised into three main areas:

Which is one of the reasons why conflict management, change management and time management are three of the most important skill areas in stress management.

Key issues in understanding Stress:

Conflict · Work-related · Damage · Demands · Pressure

Unique to the Individual · Loss · Power & Powerlessness · Change · Response

What?

WHY?

A recent report by the International Federation of Social Workers refers to the dangers of stress and burnout for social workers (ANAS 2010).

This section considers why stress is a very real issue for social work as a profession. In doing so, it explores the following questions:

- Why is it important for social workers to have a good understanding of stress and burnout?

- Why are social workers particularly vulnerable to stress?

- Why are some jobs more stress-related than others?

- Why does stress in social workers affect service users?

- Why is work-related stress so dangerous?

WHY DO I NEED TO KNOW ABOUT THIS?

Why is it important for social workers to understand stress and burnout?

It is generally agreed that social workers need to have a well-developed understanding of stress because:

- Social workers work with people who themselves are experiencing stress. The need for social workers to understand stress and stress management to work effectively with service users is now being more widely recognised

- Some research (e.g.: Rushton 1987) and social work literature (e.g.: Lloyd et al 2002) suggests that people who are more vulnerable to stress may well be more attracted to social work than other professions

Why?

- Social workers are particularly vulnerable to work-related stress and burnout

- Stress has a major impact on health and wellbeing

- Stress can impact on effective social work practice – particularly critical thinking and ethical decision making

- Understanding stress and burnout can help people to develop stress management techniques which can improve job satisfaction and effectiveness

- Service users deserve to work with social workers who have developed the skills necessary to manage stress

- Social workers experiencing stress lose their passion for social work and ultimately professional identity is eroded

Why are some jobs more stressful than others?

A range of factors make some jobs more stressful than others. Various research studies (e.g.: Maslach and Leiter 1997, Milczarek, Schneider and Gonzalez 2009) suggest the characteristics of a job which are most commonly related to workplace stress are:

- Lack of job satisfaction

- Long hours

- Lack of control

- Job insecurity

- Violence and harassment

- Poor work-life balance

- Work intensification (this refers to the speed of work expected and the imposition of deadlines)

Why?

- Lack of clarity about requirements

- Lack of team cohesion

- Overloaded work schedule

- High emotional demands at work

- Lack of support

- Lack of recognition and value

- Significant consequences when something goes wrong or mistakes are made

- Regular changes in the work environment

How many of these can be identified in social work?

- Conflict of values (particularly where a worker feels that they are being asked to do something which is unethical or against their professional values)

33

Why are social workers particularly vulnerable to stress?

Research indicates that social work is one of the occupations where work-related stress is most common (Milczarek, Schneider and Gonzalez 2009). There are various reasons for this, which might include:

- Most service users have been traumatised in some way. Secondary traumatic stress is therefore an automatic risk for social workers (almost an occupational hazard).

- Social workers are often isolated from seeking wider support – the boundaries of confidentiality mean that social workers cannot discuss the situations they encounter and the trauma that they hear about from service users with others outside of the professional environment. This can leave them more vulnerable to stress.

Why?

- Where social workers make mistakes life or death issues might be involved.

- Many of the factors which make some jobs more prone to stress than others are present in social work.

- Conflict and change are both seen as significant causes of stress. Social work almost always involves conflict at some level and certainly social work takes place in an ever changing environment.

- There are various arguments that current management approaches to social work focus on qualitative results and performance indicators which are often in conflict with social work values.

- Many of the strategies which strengthen stress resilience are reliant on a focus on self. Social workers can become so consumed by the needs of others that they fail to acknowledge the importance of focussing on themselves.

- Within the UK, at least, social workers are viewed almost entirely negatively. This creates a climate where stress can thrive.

Job demand - control model

This model devised by Karasek (1979) is perhaps the most widely used model of occupational stress. I find it particularly relevant to social work. The model is based on two dimensions to a job – how *demanding* a job is and how much *control* the person has over their own position.

In this model job control is made up of skill discretion and decision authority:

Skill discretion refers to whether a job involves a variety of tasks, low levels of repetitiveness, the use of creativity and opportunities to develop specialist skills. The opportunity to share skills with others could also be included in this section.

Decision authority refers to the worker's ability to make decisions about their own work, to influence the practice of their team and to influence wider aspects of policy and procedures.

Why?

The idea is that a job which has few demands and little control is passive; one which has low demands with high control is a low strain job. Social work is always a demanding profession - where a social worker has low levels of control the job will be 'high strain'. The usefulness of this model is explored in various parts of this guide.

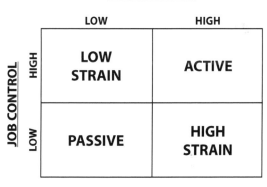

JOB DEMANDS

	LOW	HIGH
HIGH	LOW STRAIN	ACTIVE
LOW	PASSIVE	HIGH STRAIN

JOB CONTROL

Essentially, my view is that since social work will always be 'high' in terms of job demands we need to take action as social workers to ensure we have as much 'job control' as possible to ensure that we are in the 'Active' rather than 'High Strain' role.

Why does stress in social workers affect service users?

Stress and burnout in social work has an impact on service users at a range of levels:

Eborall (2003) asserts that stress in social work causes sickness absence and ultimately leads to a high staff turnover certainly in statutory social work. This leads to a shortage of staff which in turn leads to a reduced quality of care provided to service users.

Burnout in social work can leave social workers unable to empathise with service users – a quality which we know is essential to effective social work.

Research indicates that social workers who are stressed are less able to make effective and ethical critical decisions (Dolgoff et al 2008).

Why?

Social workers who experience stress are often left ineffective in their work (running around, but managing to achieve very little).

Social workers who are burnt out lack motivation and drive – both of which are needed to advocate effectively for service users.

Stress and burnout lead to social workers taking a cynical approach to their work. This can mean that service users are not viewed as unique individuals.

39

Why is work related stress so dangerous?

Work-related stress is linked to:

- Coronary heart disease
- Cardiovascular disease

- Musculoskeletal disease
- Immunological problems

- Mental health problems
- Myocardial infarction

- Hypertension
- Angina

- Stroke
- Diabetes

Why?

HOW?

In attempting to explore the question 'How can I deal with stress and burnout?' this section is based on a four R model:

Reduce	take a preventative approach to reduce the likelihood of stress having a negative impact in the first place
Recognise	watch for the signs of stress and burnout
Reverse	undo any damage which has been done by managing stress effectively and seeking support
Resilience	it is important to take care of your physical and emotional health in order to boost your resilience to stress

(adapted from the 3R model, Smith et al 2010)

Theoretically speaking there are two main approaches to dealing with stress (Lazarus and Folkman 1984, Carver, Scheier and Weintraub 1989):

Vigilant Coping also referred to as active coping or sometimes as problem solving coping. This is aimed at finding solutions to the causes of stress, and implementing the solutions – hence changing or removing the initial causes of stress. The approach focuses on changing the stressor.

Based on

Systemic model of stress

Emotion focussed Coping does not aim to change the initial causes of stress, but to find ways of managing the reactions and emotional distress caused by the situation. In this approach the stressor is not changed but the individual's response is changed.

Based on

Transactional model of stress

How?

A whole 'industry' has developed around stress and stress management. The vigilant coping model dominates this 'industry'. Most organisations therefore focus on changing the issue which is seen as creating the stress.

Social workers will always deal with difficult and stressful situations. Working with people who are disadvantaged and disenfranchised is stressful in itself. Hearing about the trauma that service users face make the work even more stressful. Therefore, many of the initial stressors facing the social work profession cannot simply be 'removed'.

Since the vigilant coping model dominates in many of the organisations which employ social workers, traditional stress management strategies which are not individualised to social work as a profession simply 'miss the mark'.

43

A combination of approaches must be used to address stress in social work. Social workers need to have uniquely developed stress management plans.

In some ways the vigilant coping and emotion focussed coping models illustrate the 'reduce' and 'resilience' aspects of the four R model. However, it is important that all four parts of the model are addressed in any stress management plan developed for social work.

Reduce

Recognise

VIGILANT COPING

Stress in Social work

EMOTION FOCUSSED COPING

Reverse

Resilience

How?

Developing a personal stress management plan

Stress is a very personal experience and what helps one person deal with stress won't necessarily work for another – so stress management plans need to be unique to every individual. In developing your own personal stress management plan you need to think about:

- **Reduce** – how can you reduce the stress in your life?

- **Recognise** – how do you know when you are stressed?

- **Reverse** – what helps you to de-stress?

- **Resilience** – how can you develop your resilience to stress?

The rest of this section should help you to develop your personal stress management plan.

Job Enrichment and Enlargement

Linking to a number of concepts covered so far in this Guide – particularly job satisfaction and job control, it is useful to consider job enrichment and enlargement which was first written about by Porter et al (1982). The model outlines how job satisfaction impacts on motivation. We also know that job satisfaction affects stress levels.

Porter et al argue that when people have been in the same role for some time, their satisfaction in the role may reduce. The model describes how this can be addressed by either job enlargement or job enrichment.

Job Enlargement refers to extending the scope of a role by combining two or more roles, giving a greater variety and a more 'holistic' feel. For example, a social worker who takes on the role of practice educator is 'enlarging' their role and is therefore likely to increase their job satisfaction. It is important to recognise that job enlargement does not necessarily mean taking more on in terms of workload – it is more about carrying out different types of work.

How?

Job Enrichment refers to people having more responsibilities to set their own pace, deciding their own methods, correcting their own 'mistakes' etc. Job enrichment results in greater autonomy by giving people more control over their own work.

Both job enrichment and job enlargement relate closely to Karasek's (1979) job demand – control model. Job enrichment can provide enhanced skill discretion and job enlargement improves decision authority. Both are therefore methods which can be used to take a social worker into the 'active' (least stressful) role in Karasek's model.

Some of the work currently taking place within the profession on developing career pathways for social workers builds on the concept of job enrichment and job enlargement.

Many employers refer to difficulties in recruiting and retaining experienced social workers. Looking at the roles on offer in terms of enriching and enlarging them is seen as an effective way of encouraging experienced practitioners to remain in practice whilst avoiding burnout.

How do I reduce the likelihood of stress having a negative impact?

Everyone's experience of stress is unique. So the best methods to prevent stress will be completely personal to that individual. However, there are some methods of stress prevention that everyone could explore:

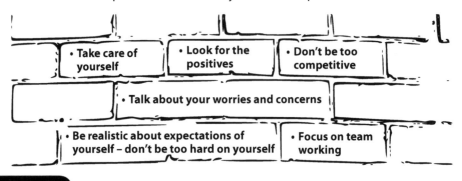

- Take care of yourself
- Look for the positives
- Don't be too competitive
- Talk about your worries and concerns
- Be realistic about expectations of yourself – don't be too hard on yourself
- Focus on team working

How?

Top Tips

The International Stress Management Association (2009) recommend the following top ten tips for avoiding stress:

1. Learn to manage your time more effectively
2. Adopt a healthy lifestyle
3. Know your limitations and don't take too much on
4. Find out what causes you stress
5. Avoid unnecessary conflict
6. Accept the things you cannot change
7. Take time out to relax and recharge your batteries
8. Find time to meet friends
9. Try to see things differently, develop a positive thinking style
10. Avoid alcohol, nicotine and caffeine as coping mechanisms

Stress SWOT analysis

SWOT analysis is an audit tool widely used in strategic planning where a decision is required. It is a method often used in marketing or business. Since it is an evaluation tool, it can be a useful technique for social workers to explore the potential for stress and to begin to develop a personal stress prevention plan:

Strengths refers to factors such as capabilities, resources and advantages. Think about your personal strengths, your support networks, resources that you can draw on etc. To carry out a Stress SWOT analysis you should think about everything that you can draw on to help you manage stress effectively.

How?

Weakness refers to areas that you are not so good at, areas of resource scarcity and areas of vulnerability. Try to reflect on all the areas that you need to change in your life, including new skills that you need to develop. Think about your learning needs, where there are gaps in your personal resources, negative situations you find yourself in and any problems you are experiencing.

Opportunities refers to things which can exploit the identified strengths or address the identified weaknesses. Work your way through your strengths and think about how you can build on these and maximise them. Work through the weaknesses and consider what you might be able to do about them.

Threats refers to things that might cause damage, that might feed into the weaknesses identified and undermine the strengths. When identifying threats consider the consequences of not addressing the weaknesses you have identified and think about the dangers that might occur if you do not effectively manage the stress.

51

Employer responsibilities in reducing the risk of stress to employees

It is generally accepted that employers have a responsibility to reduce the risk of stress to employees. The International Federation of Social Workers recommends that employers of social workers *"should take into account this occupational hazard, analyse its cause and identify ways of minimising risks."* (ANAS 2010: 2)

In the UK, health and safety legislation places a responsibility on employers to protect the health and safety of their employees. Recognising the extent of work-related stress and the need to support organisations to meet their responsibilities, the Health and Safety Executive has produced a set of management standards which provide a five stage approach for organisations to minimise the risk of work-related stress:

How?

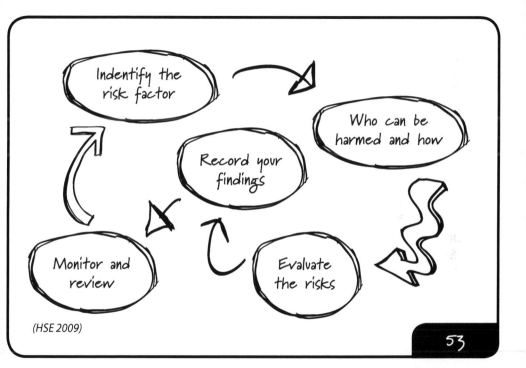

Indentify the risk factor

Who can be harmed and how

Record your findings

Monitor and review

Evaluate the risks

(HSE 2009)

53

The HSE Management Standards identify six areas of work design which are the primary source of stress at work. The management standards are written around these six areas:

Demands

this covers issues such as workload, work pattern and environment. The standards include - *people's skills and abilities are matched to their job demands.*

Control

this refers to how much control a person has over their own work. The standards include - *employees are consulted over their work patterns.*

Support

this is about the support, encouragement and resources provided by the organisation, the line manager and colleagues. The standards include - *employees know what support is available and how and when to access it.*

How?

Relationships — this is about the need for positive working relationships. The standards include – *the organisation promotes positive behaviours at work to avoid conflict and ensure fairness.*

Role — refers to whether a person understands their role within an organisation and how the organisation ensures that they do not have conflicting roles. The standards include – *the organisation ensures that as far as possible, the different requirements it places upon employees are compatible.*

Change — refers to the way that organisational change is managed and communicated within the organisation. The standards include – *employees are given necessary training to support any changes in their job.*

Talking about Stress

Talking about the factors that create stress and your responses can be helpful for a range of reasons:

Raising the issue means that people become aware of your needs for support

It can help to get the issue into perspective. Sometimes when you say something out loud you begin to wonder why it became such a big issue for you

Talking to others often helps you to find a solution for yourself

Informal support groups can be instigated by talking things through

How?

However helpful talking about stress is, people are often reluctant to talk about stress at work. They believe that there is a stigma related to it and that if others around them are coping they should be able to "cope" too. There is a fear that people who talk about stress at work will be seen as weak and unable to cope. It is however, vital to recognise that stress is not a sign of weakness – we can all be affected by it. Very often, when one person in a team begins to talk about the stress they are experiencing, all those who seem to be "coping" open up about their concerns too.

57

Looking After Yourself

There is a tendency for people in the caring professions to define themselves only in terms of what they do for others. They remain so focused on the needs of others that they have little energy left for themselves, many of the social workers I work with feel that to focus on themselves is selfish or self-centred.

However, self care is an essential aspect of stress management. Self neglect leads to poor health, problems in relationships and ultimately has a huge impact on personal and professional effectiveness. Looking after yourself is therefore an essential aspect of being a good social worker.

THE WAY IN WHICH WE LOOK AFTER OURSELVES WILL BE UNIQUE TO EACH OF US

How?

Looking after yourself effectively includes:

- Taking a break for lunch (away from your desk)

- Taking thirty minutes for yourself three times a week (doing anything that is just for you)

- Being attuned to your own needs

- Being clear about your own boundaries

- Not being too hard on yourself

- Staying true to your own values

- Making healthy lifestyle choices

You won't be effective in meeting other peoples needs unless you address your own!

Keeping it 'real'

Social workers can be very self-critical. Some are clearly perfectionists. Whilst we all want to do the best job we can, it is important that we don't place even more demands on ourselves.

Perhaps social workers are so self-critical because reflective practice and taking a critical approach to this is so integral to social work, or maybe it's because social work as a profession is criticised so heavily. Whatever the reason, being *overly* self-critical will add to the stress we experience. Being realistic about what can be achieved, whilst always striving for best practice is important.

Many of the models we have explored make it clear that stress is caused by demands. These demands are not always external. Social workers who are too self-critical place further demands on themselves.

How?

McKinnon (1998) claims that helping professionals often cause stress by their own expectations. Social workers often expect the impossible of themselves.

Certainly, those social workers who accept that "I can only do what I can do" deal with stress much more effectively.

It is important to be critically reflective and to constantly review how we can improve our practice. However, to avoid stress and burnout it is vital to keep things 'real' and ensure the balance is right. Remember to also reflect on what you do well.

IT'S IMPORTANT TO GET THE BALANCE RIGHT

Positive Thinking

A whole industry has built itself up around the power of positive thinking. Perhaps it is because we are so surrounded by the importance of it, that we often overlook the relevance of positive thinking.

Henry Ford is attributed with saying....
"If you think you can or you think you can't …. You're right!"

Negative	**Realistic**	**Positive**
It will **never** happen	It **could** happen	It **will** happen

How?

Negative thinking certainly creates stress. Positive thinking can both reduce the likelihood of stress and help address stressful situations.

There are three stages to positive thinking:

Thought awareness – it is important to become aware of your thoughts, particularly negative thoughts.

Rational thinking – negative thoughts should be challenged. Question the thought. Is it really factual? If it is a fact then learn from it. If, as is more likely, it is not a fact then refute the thought as untrue.

Positive affirmation – replace the negative thought with a positive.

63

REBT and CBT

Rational Emotive Behaviour Therapy (REBT) and Cognitive Behavioural Therapy (CBT) are regularly referred to in social work. Many social workers use the models or at least aspects of them in their work with service users but they fail to see the relevance to themselves. Both these approaches have the concept of positive thinking at their core, so they can be helpful in considering how social workers can develop more positive thinking to address stress.

Drawn from a combination of these approaches, the ABCDEF model (Ellis 1962) is helpful in considering how we can develop positive thinking:

How?

A Activating Experience

B What **B**eliefs the person has about themselves as a result of A

C The **C**onsequences to the person

REBT and CBT are about unpicking the negative beliefs that people have, so the model then moves on to look at how individuals can:

D **D**ispute the beliefs and question whether they are rational

E Replace the irrational belief with an **E**ffective rational belief

F Replace the **F**eelings which will be the result of the negative belief

65

A key component of CBT is the concept of "self talk". We need to understand the though processes that develop the negative thought and then provide ourselves with a "voice within" which challenge the negativity, replacing it with a positive thought...

How?

Visualisation & Positive Thinking

Some people find visualisation useful in promoting positive thinking. Visualisation is often seen as a useful stress buster. Two social workers I know share their methods of visualisation:

> I find somewhere quiet (often my car) and think of a time in my life I was happy and relaxed. For me it was a particular holiday in Texas when we stayed in a wooden house that we dubbed 'Little House on the Prairie'. I imagine myself sitting in a rocking chair on the veranda watching the sunset and listening to the birds singing. This quickly calms and relaxes me. I find it really helps at those time when I feel so stressed I can't think straight.

Angela Hassall

> When I feel really stressed I picture Irena Sendler. She was an amazing woman. A social worker in Warsaw, Poland at the time of the Nazi occupation. She worked hard with her colleagues to move 2,500 children out of the ghetto and into safety. It wasn't until 1999 that her work was recognised. The recognition came as a surprise to Irena who saw herself as "just a social worker". Picturing Irena and thinking of her struggles puts my own stress into perspective. It gives me inspiration to continue and a pride in my professional history.

Karen Peers

Develop a "Mantra"

Mantras originated in India and are now used in various spiritual and faith movements – such as Buddhism, Sikhism and Jainism. The idea of a mantra is that a phrase considered capable of creating a transformation is consistently repeated. It can be useful as a method of 'self talk' to create positive thinking and a sense of calm. The 'mantra' can be anything which the individual finds useful. I find my personal 'mantra' very useful in relieving stress and increasing my personal motivation. I first heard it as part of Gary Bailey's inaugural speech as the President of the International Federation of Social Workers (2010) and I've often repeated it to myself since then:

**"Life is not about waiting for the storm to pass.
It's about learning to dance in the rain."**

How?

It struck a particular chord with me because there is always a 'storm' of some kind in social work. It's all too easy to think "if I keep my head down and say nothing, it'll go away". It simply never does "go away". Waiting for the storm to pass can leave a social worker at best ineffectual; at worst significantly stressed and possibly burnt out. Learning how to dance in the rain however, is challenging but exciting and fun.

The team I work with often refer to the mantra – when we are facing something particularly challenging, we refer to learning how to dance in the rain. It can provide a useful focus for discussion and team building.

Top Tips for Positive Thinking

Social workers work in very difficult situations. This can mean they find positive thinking more difficult. In the current climate of scarce resources social workers very often find themselves having to focus on the negatives at work. Simply to obtain basic services or to justify any form of intervention the worst possible picture has to be painted. So whilst some of the following tips might sound very trite – do think about them carefully. Do you *really* adopt a positive thinking style? It is all about your choices.

- Smile regularly.
  Develop your sense of humour.

- List the positives in your life –
  think about everything good.

- Try positive visualisation.

> Social work in the current climate can create a negative thinking pattern. We need to actively consider how to develop and maintain positive thinking.

How?

- List the negatives – don't dwell on what they are but rather think about which ones you can change immediately, which ones you can change in the longer term, and accept those things which you cannot change.

- Let go of any negative feelings you have towards someone else – the negative thoughts hurt you more than anyone else.

- Surround yourself with positivity – listen to positive music, watch positive films, look at positive images. The impact of the senses on your mood and thought processes cannot be underestimated.

- Maintain a solution focussed approach in your practice.

- Consider social work approaches which have a positive view - such as strengths perspectives.

- Look for the opportunities in every difficulty.

- Take pride in being a social worker.

71

Appreciating the small things

The issues which social workers work with are often entrenched over a number of years and generally involve a range of complex factors. It can be easy to lose sight of achievements and positive change within this. Sometimes peoples needs and difficulties are so significant that small achievements are not recognised. However it is important to recognise that complex and difficult situations will not change overnight.

An important aspect of addressing stress is to notice and appreciate every step that is taken - every positive in the work you do.

"Every journey begins with a single step"
(McKinnon 1998)

How?

Satisfaction as a stress reducer

Research clearly demonstrates that job satisfaction is one of the most effective defences against stress (Collins 2007). Stamm (2009) proposes a 'theory of compassion satisfaction' which explores the way that satisfaction at work supports a worker to avoid stress and burnout.

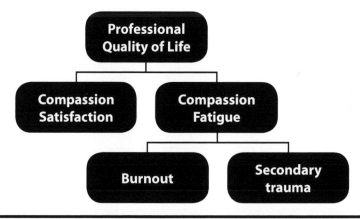

Compared with other occupations, social workers have reported high levels of job satisfaction. One survey in 2003 found that social work was in the top twenty occupations enjoying high levels of job satisfaction (Rose 2003). It is clear, however, that social workers find some aspects of their job very satisfying (generally contact with service users) and other aspects much less so (often government directives and agency policy and procedure) (Jones 2001).

In order to prevent burnout and chronic stress the friedsocialworker.com (2009) recommends that social workers should keep a satisfaction survey. This should record every aspect of work and the working environment with which you are satisfied, and it should be regularly reviewed over time:

Research indicates that social workers who understand their 'core' (why they came into social work) and who are clear about what they enjoy about the work are those social workers who have the strongest resilience to stress. (Grant and Kinman 2009).

How?

I am satisfied with........	I am satisfied because........	Nov 2010	Feb 2011	May 2011
Weekly peer supervision	Useful to de-brief and to reflect on practice	Yes	Not happening	Not happening
Contact with service users	I feel that I am really making a difference	Yes	Yes	Yes
New recording requirements	Much clearer and less bureaucratic than previous system	Yes	Yes	Yes - the recent changes have improved it further

It is vitally important that the satisfaction survey is positively framed and focuses on what you are satisfied with rather than on what you are dissatisfied with. Reflecting on satisfaction levels is likely to reduce stress whereas focussing on dissatisfaction may well increase levels of stress.

Time Management

One of the most significant causes of stress for social workers is the feeling of pressure due to a lack of time. Undoubtedly case loads are high and time is very pressured.

It can feel like an easy 'opt out' of responsibility when managers and employers say that developing time management skills is an effective stress management method. However, developing skills in time management certainly does assist in managing stress more effectively.

Every social worker will be in a very different position in terms of prioritising and time management issues – so again time management improvements must be uniquely considered. All that can be given in a book of this kind is some basic advice on effective time management.

How?

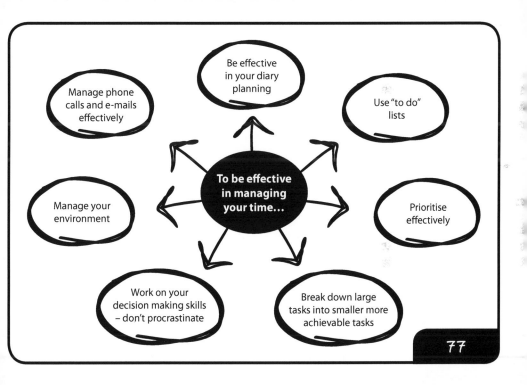

Manage phone calls and e-mails effectively

Be effective in your diary planning

Use "to do" lists

Manage your environment

To be effective in managing your time…

Prioritise effectively

Work on your decision making skills – don't procrastinate

Break down large tasks into smaller more achievable tasks

77

To Do Lists

Many people find 'To Do' lists (sometimes referred to as Task Lists) very useful tools in terms of time management. They are also useful as 'stress-busters' because many people find ticking things off a list very satisfying and helpful in minimising feelings of pressure and stress.

If you're not used to using 'To Do' lists, you may find the following guidance useful:

✓ You may want to develop one general 'To Do' list – or a number of 'To Do' lists (for example, a list for each case you are working on). Whatever method you chose, it is important that you don't just end up with lots of lists.

✓ Each task on the list should take no more than one to two hours (break down larger tasks).

How?

✓ Lists should indicate which tasks are the highest priority.

✓ 'To Do' lists must be kept up to date – the most effective aspect of such lists in terms of stress management is ticking things off when they are done.

✓ If you find you often think of things you need to do at work when you are elsewhere (even just as you are falling asleep) keep a small notepad and pen to hand so that you can jot down the things to be done, as you remember them.

✓ Some people find that indicating deadlines for each task is helpful.

✓ Maintain flexibility.

✓ A whole variety of methods for keeping 'To Do' lists - online methods, or electronic methods (on phones for example) are now available. Look for a method which suits you.

Don't take too much on

Perhaps one of the most regular complaints that social workers make is about the amount of work that they have. Recognising that managers are under pressure to allocate, that there are deadlines and that service users have needs which cannot necessarily wait, social workers often take too much on. If you do take too much on, you will not be able to manage all the competing demands effectively and you will increase the amount of stress you are under.

McGregor (2010) offers the following advice about how to turn down unreasonable work requests:

- Know when you have reached your limit
- Manage your own feelings
- Be assertive
- Prepare in advance

How?

Saying "No"

If you feel that you are at your working capacity and you need to say 'No' to the allocation of further work, it's worth working through this step by step so that you can address this effectively.

So when your manager asks you to take on more work:

1. Show that you have heard them.

> I recognise that you want me to take on two more assessments.

2. Show empathy with their position.

> I understand that you have to allocate these cases to meet deadlines.

3. Explain your position clearly.

> However, I am at capacity at the moment. I simply cannot take on any more work. I would be likely to make mistakes and certainly deadlines would not be met.

4. Provide an option.

> I should be able to complete the assessment for the Stepping family this week. Once that has been agreed and signed I will be able to take one of the referrals – so we can talk about it again on Friday...

How?

But it's just not that easy!

As a social worker writing this Pocket Guide, I recognise that some of the advice isn't that easy to put into practice. The whole aspect of saying 'no' to further work is perhaps going to be the hardest thing. It is however, really important that you work on this area. Whilst the four step process might sound trite, it really does work. Try it.

"What if my manager doesn't accept no for an answer?"

If the four step process doesn't work, you have a few options, but perhaps the most important thing to remember is that you should only 'own' your own stress – don't take your manager's stress on board. They need to find their way of addressing this.

Don't give in to emotional extortion "you're the only worker I can ask to take this on, it's so important..." etc. You need to protect your ability to work effectively with the other work you have allocated.

If your manager refuses to take no for an answer and still feels you should be taking more work on, make a formal request for a meeting. Ask your manager to go through your workload with you, advising on how you can take on more whilst maintaining quality and effectiveness. Ensure that everything is recorded.

Email your thoughts to your manager. Be clear about why you cannot take on more work. Spell out your workload, state that you have concerns about your ability to manage effectively if you take on more work - use the four stage process in the email.

Keep a record of the time spent on different activities and ask your manager to advise on which activities should 'go' to allow you to take on more work. You need to be able to provide a clear evidence base rather than simply saying "I've got too much on."

Social workers do have a great deal on - but likewise as a profession we need to make clear what is workable and what isn't. If you have too high workload look at your own role in this.

How?

Conflict and Stress

Conflict and stress are closely linked such that there is an element of chicken and egg – what comes first?

- Conflict is certainly a major cause of stress

- Stress can leave people unable to manage conflict – the way that people behave when they are stressed can even create conflict

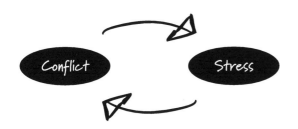

Conflict → Stress

Conflict is very often viewed wholly negatively. However, it is important to recognise that conflict can actually be a positive experience – many people learn and grow from their experiences of conflict.

If stress is always viewed negatively it will be seen as a threat – in which case a stress reaction is more likely to kick in and the conflict will be more difficult to deal with.

Conflict is a fact of life so learning how to deal with conflict rather than avoiding it is crucial – it is after all impossible to sweep everything under the carpet. It will catch you out at some point!

How?

Segal and Smith (2010) state that the ability to successfully resolve conflict relies on your ability to:

Control your emotions

Pay attention to feelings (yours and others)

Recognise and respond to the things that matter to the other person

React in a calm, non-defensive, respectful way

Seek out compromise

notice how many of these are affected by stress?

87

Conflict Management

Thomas and Kilmann (1974) identified five different ways of approaching conflict:

Avoidance

Characteristics	Unassertive, uncooperative
Actions	Flee, deny, ignore, withdraw
Might be appropriate when	The issue is trivial
Is not appropriate when	The issue is important. It is used as the usual method of dealing with conflict. Negativity might linger

"Conflict? What Conflict?"

How?

Accommodation

Characteristics	Unassertive, cooperative
Actions	Agree, appease
Might be appropriate when	The issue isn't important. You recognise you are wrong. It's your 'turn' to back down
Is not appropriate when	You will resent it. You use this as a regular method to be accepted by others

"Whatever you want is ok with me"

Competition

Characteristics	Assertive (possibly aggressive), uncooperative
Actions	Competing, controlling, fight, coerce
Might be appropriate when	There is an emergency and a rapid decision is required
Is not appropriate when	It is used to bully people

"It's my way or the highway"

How?

Compromise

Characteristics	Partly assertive and partly cooperative
Actions	Bargain, negotiate something for everyone
Might be appropriate when	Finding a solution is important. Cooperation is important but time and resources are limited
Is not appropriate when	You can't live with the consequences

"Let's split the difference"

Collaboration

Characteristics	Assertive, Cooperative
Actions	Gather information, explore all the options, be creative, discuss with others
Might be appropriate when	There is some hope that all the concerns can be addressed. The relationships involved are important
Is not appropriate when	Time is short. The issues aren't really important

"How can we work together to solve this problem?"

 How?

As a social worker you are likely to experience conflict in a range of different relationships. For example, social workers may well be in conflict with service users and/or their carers or with other professionals or with decision-makers in the organisation.

The reason for the conflict and the nature of the conflict is likely to differ as the role, responsibilities and boundaries vary in the different relationships. Therefore, the most appropriate conflict management approach will differ in the variety of situations and relationships which social workers find themselves in.

It is therefore very useful for social workers to have a range of conflict management approaches in their 'skill box'.

The 5 A Approach to Conflict

Borisoff and Victor (1998) identified five stages to conflict resolution:

Assessment
In this stage the parties involved gather information to decide on the problem. They agree on the central nature of the problem and decide on which conflict management method would work best. Each party indicates what they want to achieve and where they might compromise.

Acknowledgement
Here each party listens to the other. Active listening is really important and each person should indicate to the other that they have heard what is being said – even if they don't agree with it.

How?

Attitude

This involves acknowledging diversity and the impact that culture and stereotyping might have on the situation. Any potential problems arising from difference should be explored.

Action

The parties implement the chosen model for resolving the conflict.

Analysis

Everyone involved agrees what they will do as the outcome of the discussions. A clear summary is needed and an agreement should be made about what will happen in the future. The short term and long term results will be evaluated.

Responding to Change

Social work operates in an ever changing world. This can add to the stress that social workers experience as they can feel that they just begin to understand something and then it changes. Some people relish change, others dread it. You need to be aware of your own responses to change. When you hear the word 'change', how does it make you feel?

> "It's not the strongest of the species that survives, or the most intelligent, but the one the most responsive to change."
>
> (Source unknown).

It is important that you are aware of your response to change. If you have a feeling of dread or fear about change then you are more likely to experience stress as a result of the change. If you look forward to the challenge of change then you are likely to be able to view change positively.

How?

Anticipating Change

Social workers need to be clear about change in a range of areas:

- What changes they need to make to their own practice

- What changes need to be made to the team or service in which they work

- What changes are coming

You may think that to anticipate change, you need a crystal ball. However, in many ways when social workers keep up to date and employ evidence based practice they are able to anticipate change. At the very least, you can be certain that there will be change!

Kotter's Model

There are various theories and models around change management. Most of these focus on how change should be managed within organisations. Perhaps the most well known model is Kotter's eight step model (eg: 2002).

| Increase urgency | Build the Guiding Team | Get the vision right | Communicate effectively |

| Make change stick | Don't let up | Create short term wins (achievable goals) | Empower action |

How?

Since models of change predominately focus on how managers and organisations should manage change, it is easy to 'blame' when stress is caused by change. However, everyone needs to take responsibility and play their part in change management. The responsibility of individuals in managing change is now more widely acknowledged. Capstick (2010) recommends that to manage change effectively, people need to:

- Anticipate change accurately

- Keep positive about change

- Take care of their physical and emotional health

- Use relaxation techniques

- Keep an open mind

- Gradually build up the change

- Ensure support is located

- Keep a sense of humour

How many of these are also strategies for managing stress?

How do I recognise the signs of stress?

It is important to be fully aware of the signs and symptoms of stress, as covered on pages 23-25. However, when people are experiencing chronic stress or burnout they are often unable to recognise the signs of stress in themselves.

It is much more likely that those around you will recognise the signs of stress and the changes in your behaviour.

How?

McKinnon (1998: 2) suggests that there are a range of warning signs that someone is experiencing "dangerous levels" of stress:

 Thinking you are indispensable

 Negative thinking

 Extreme, exaggerated or misplaced emotional reactions

 Getting away physically but not mentally

 Fatigue and lack of energy

 Frequent illness

 Poor relationships

101

Keeping a Stress Diary

It is useful to keep a record of stress as you experience it – although this need not necessarily be kept in a diary form. The record can help give an insight into your own reactions and can provide a clear benchmark against which you can measure any significant changes. The record must be kept under regular review if it is to be of any use.

Various methods can be used to keep the 'stress diary'. It could be as simple as, for example, taking the list of stress signs and symptoms on page 23 - 25 or the list of warning signs on page 99 and adding a tick or cross each month. How many crosses do you get? At what point do you decide you are experiencing a dangerous level of stress?

Or you could try writing a 'free narrative' or reflective account once a week or fortnight or month about your feelings, focussing on any issues relating to stress levels. Keep any significant changes under review.

How?

Am I in control of stress or is stress controlling me?

Remember, the aim is not to eradicate stress – the aim is to use stress positively and to ensure that you are controlling stress rather than the other way around. So as part of keeping your stress diary regularly ask yourself:

- When I feel agitated, do I know how to quickly calm and soothe myself?

- Can I easily let go of my anger?

- Can I turn to others to help me calm down and feel better?

- When my energy is low can I boost it easily?

- Do I often feel tense or tight somewhere in my body?

- Does conflict absorb my time and attention?

(adapted from Segal 2008 and Segal and Smith 2010)

103

'Stress busting' support

Widely recognised as one of the most useful coping mechanisms to address stress, support can be provided in a range of ways.

In social work, specifically, support is seen as one of the most important aspects to effective stress management. Collins (2007) identified the following coping strategies as the most useful in social work:

- Social support – predominantly support from friends and family

- Support from colleagues

- Good quality supportive supervision

Social workers need to identify their support networks, build on them and accept the support offered

How?

Scaffolding Support

Support from colleagues who share experiences is undoubtedly one of the most effective methods of addressing stress for social workers. This support can be provided in a range of formal or informal ways through:

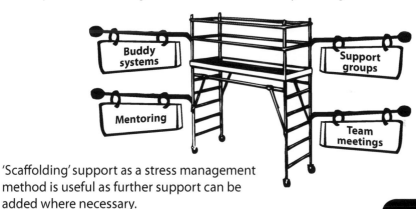

Buddy systems

Support groups

Mentoring

Team meetings

'Scaffolding' support as a stress management method is useful as further support can be added where necessary.

Mentoring

Mentoring has a long history. The word itself is drawn from ancient mythology – when Odysseus went to Troy, he left mentor to be a "trusted friend and adviser" to his son. Since then, the word has been used to describe a relationship where one person who is more experienced than another takes on a role to assist, support and advise another.

Traditionally, people have always sought informal mentors. For example, when a person is experiencing something new, they may approach a worker they trust and whose practice they respect, to ask questions etc. In this way, they are seeking an informal mentor.

Many organisations have begun to recognise the value of mentoring and have set up formalised mentoring schemes, where workers new to a particular team, role or task are linked with a more experienced worker who will act as a mentor.

How?

If you are asked to take on the role of mentor, you might feel that this will simply add to your workload and therefore increase stress. However, becoming a mentor can make you feel positive about yourself, can increase satisfaction and can vary your working day, increasing motivation and reducing stress. Referring back to the job demand control model acting as mentor can increase job control (both through skill discretion and decision authority). It is well worth thinking about taking on a mentoring role – either formally or informally.

Having a mentor prevents stress

Mentoring

Being a mentor prevents stress

Support Groups

Many social work organisations have support groups for specific groups of workers (often those who are more likely to face discrimination and oppression in society) such as Black workers, workers with disabilities, workers of specific genders or sexuality etc. Research shows that where social workers are a part of these groups they are likely to find them useful in combatting stress.

More recently, action learning sets are being used for social workers undertaking specific qualifications, or those with specific job roles (Newly Qualified Social Workers often experience action learning sets as a part of the support offered to them). Research has demonstrated that these are useful in providing mutual support for social workers – and providing support against stress (Coulshed and Mullender 2006).

How?

Team Relationships

Teams can be a supportive haven or a breeding ground for further stress. To work effectively social workers need to be 'team players'. However, we all know there are some people who can make us feel even more stressed. Swinton (2010) refers to 'stress sneezers' – people who sneeze out stress germs and pass their stress to others (often feeling better themselves in the process). It is useful to take some time to reflect on the dynamics in your team and to work out who are. The 'stress sneezers' in the team.

ATISHOOOOOOOO

Team Meetings

Team meetings are a vital forum in terms of stress management. However, many social workers report that team meetings are overtaken by discussions about bureaucratic matters, case allocation and routines (Collins 2007). Some team meetings simply provide a forum for the 'stress sneezers' in a team to hit a wider audience.

Take the chance to discuss team meeting agendas with your team and the team manager and make sure that more time is allowed for support issues and discussion about difficulties which focuses on reflection and solutions. Ensure that team meetings are used as an opportunity to celebrate good practice and professional identity.

How?

"Our team meetings used to be stressful in themselves. They just became a 'moaning shop'. We agreed to change the format and now I find them really supportive. One meeting focusses on 'business' matters like policy changes, updates on local resources and service changes. The next meeting focuses on practice issues. We take it in turns to bring a piece of work we want to discuss and use it as an opportunity for reflection. At least one 'success story' is also shared in each team meeting, reminding us of the good work we do."

Supervision

It is commonly acknowledged (e.g.: Morrison 2005) that there are four functions to supervision in social work and social care:

Accountability Function
Sometimes referred to as the managerial or normative function, this is about the supervisor ensuring that the worker's practice is competent.

Developmental Function
Sometimes referred to as the educative function, this is about the role of supervision in helping promote a worker's continuing professional development.

How?

Supportive Function
Sometimes referred to as the restorative function, this covers the role which supervisors have to value those they supervise and to provide the necessary professional support.

Mediation Function
This is about engaging the individual with the organisation – ensuring that organisational requirements are clear, clarifying any ambiguities and addressing competing demands.

Despite the fact that supervision has these four functions, many social workers experience poor quality supervision which focuses almost entirely on the allocation of work. However, all the recent reports into social work in England have highlighted the vital importance of supervision to effective social work practice so it is likely that these experiences are set to change.

Kadushin (1992) recognised that supervision should provide a forum to remove a worker from stress and provide an opportunity for discussion about stress.

The role of good quality professional supervision in addressing stress in social work is once again becoming more widely recognised. Jones (2011: 19) makes clear that:

"One of the requirements in the social work role is to stay close to, and empathetic with, people at times of stress and pain. At times all of this can be overwhelming .... Supervision should provide a safe and secure space for these stresses and strains to be shared with the supervisor, as well as reflected and acted upon".

Social work practitioners should ensure that they make use of supervision to explore the stress they are experiencing.

How?

The final report of the Social Work Taskforce highlighted the importance of effective supervision in providing the environment required for effective social work practice.

At the time of writing, the Social Work Reform Board is developing a supervision framework. This refers to the need for regular supervision (at least monthly) provided by registered social workers who have received supervision training. This supervision should cover the following four areas (reflecting the functions of supervision).

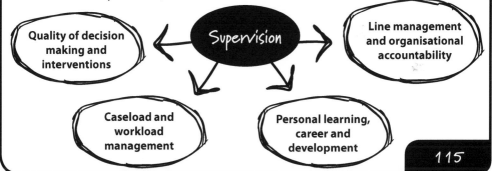

Quality of decision making and interventions

Supervision

Line management and organisational accountability

Caseload and workload management

Personal learning, career and development

Continuing Professional Development

When work demands are high, one of the first things social workers sacrifice is their own CPD. How many times have you been aware, for example, of social workers called back from training or from another learning activity to deal with a crisis on their caseload? Personally, I have worked with a number of social workers who haven't completed qualifications because of the pressures they face at work. This is a mistake.

Taking a proactive stance to your own learning and professional development is an effective stress management strategy for a range of reasons, which include:

- It enables reflection which can help identify satisfaction with the role

- It encourages skill development which is a key aspect of job 'control' (Karasek 1979)

- It can refresh your 'core' as a social worker

How?

- It improves understanding of change and therefore assists in change management

Despite the importance of CPD, social workers do often let it go and get pulled into different areas – this reflects social workers common reluctance to look after themselves (see page 58). However, it is vital that you do maintain your CPD and that you place a priority on this.

Try the following:

- Don't think of CPD activities just as training – look for the full range of active opportunities

- Ensure you play an active part in making your supervision a learning activity

- Think about sharing your practice wisdom in a variety of ways

- Recognise the value of CPD in terms of stress management

Reversing the damage

Smith et al (2010) use the analogy of driving to explain three main ways of responding to stress:

- Foot on the accelerator: this is angry or agitated stress where a person is seemingly unable to sit still.

- Foot on the brake: a withdrawn or depressed stress response. Here people shut down and show very little energy or emotion.

- Foot on both: a mixture of the two this is a tense and frozen response. Here the person freezes under pressure so that they are unable to do anything. The person looks paralysed but under the surface they are extremely agitated.

How?

In fact none of these approaches is useful in responding to stress. So if you find yourself responding to stress in one of these ways, reverse and try to look at the situation differently. In this way, hopefully any damage caused by the stress can be reversed.

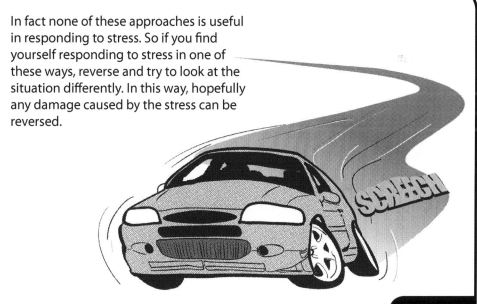

Complimentary Therapies and Approaches

Also referred to as holistic therapies or alternative therapies, many people find that complimentary health approaches are helpful to them. In terms of the four R model complimentary therapies can be used in a range of ways. For example in:

- Promoting relaxation and **reducing** the likelihood of stress having a negative impact

- Providing a forum where stress can be **recognised**

- **Reversing** any damage done by stressful experiences

- Promoting **resilience** to stress

How?

There are a vast range of complimentary approaches. Some of the most popular are:

Hypnotherapy - this explores how the power of the mind can be unlocked to make changes. It is seen as particularly helpful in addressing problematic responses to stress

Aromatherapy - the use of essential oils is said to be particularly effective in relieving stress

Crystal therapy

Alexander technique

Autogenic training - training in self-hypnosis, this can be useful in supporting people to develop deeper relaxation

Reflexology

Reiki

Acupuncture

Homeopathy

Yoga - is seen as a useful technique to support both physical and mental relaxation

Meditation - there are a number of techniques to support meditation which can support relaxation and positive thinking

Stress Aid kits

First aid kits are an essential requirement in every workplace and we all know how important they are in terms of health and safety. A stress aid kit builds on this idea. A personal stress aid kit should be made up of things which a person finds helpful in combatting or addressing stress. So for example, your stress aid kit might include:

- Favourite music CD

- A DVD which you enjoy

- Something which encourages you to take time for yourself doing something you enjoy – it might be something as simple as some bubble bath

How?

A Healthy Lifestyle

Stress creates a range of physical responses. Perhaps the best way to build resilience to stress is to take a physical approach and to lead a healthy lifestyle. Often described as one of the best defences against stress, a healthy lifestyle involves:

- Healthy eating
- Regular exercise
- Sleep and rest
- Healthy drinking
- Not smoking
- Balanced lifestyle

How?

Tips for Healthy Eating

The Food Standards Agency gives the following 8 tips for eating well:

1. Base meals on starchy foods

2. Eat lots of fruit and vegetables

3. Eat more fish

4. Cut down on saturated fat and sugar

5. Try to eat less salt – no more than 6g a day

6. Get active and try to stick to a healthy weight

7. Drink plenty of water

8. Don't skip breakfast

Whilst this is very basic advice, you should review it.

Busy social workers often 'skip' a number of these tips in practice.

Regular exercise

Regular exercise is one of the most essential components of a healthy lifestyle. In fact a review of the major research in recent years has concluded that other than not smoking, regular exercise is the most important factor in a healthy lifestyle (Alford 2010). In addition to promoting resilience to stress by contributing to a healthy lifestyle, exercise can help address stress because it produces endorphins – the body's natural 'feel good' chemicals.

When planning your exercise think about FIT:

F frequency: how often will you exercise?

I intensity: how intense will the exercise be?

T type: what type of exercise will you do?

How?

Avoiding 'Bad Habits'

Many people turn to what could be referred to as 'false friends' when they are experiencing stress. For example, some people will increase their drinking, some people will smoke, people might turn to prescription or non-prescription drugs etc.

It is however clear, that all of these actions actually make stress reactions worse. They may give some short term relief, but in the longer term alcohol use or reliance on nicotine or other substances will make the process of stress defence and stress management much more difficult (Wilkinson 2003).

"ALCOHOL & NICOTINE ARE LIKELY TO ADD TO STRESS"

Sleep and Stress

A lack of sleep and stress are interrelated in that:

- a lack of sufficient sleep can make us more prone to stress

- sleep disturbance is a common symptom of stress

Most adults need around eight hours of sleep per night to function effectively. This is not easy if you are experiencing stress. To manage stress it is important to develop positive sleeping habits.

| Lack of sleep | Causes | Stress | Causes | Sleep disturbance |

The vicious 'sleep & stress' cycle

How?

Different things work for different people but the following tips can assist in getting a good night's sleep:

- Set a regular bedtime and stick to it

- Get up at the same time every day – if you go to bed late one night make sure you still get up at the usual time

- Keep your bedroom dark and cool

- Make sure your bed is comfortable

- Use relaxation techniques

- Don't eat late at night

- Take regular exercise

Relaxing bedtime rituals might include:

- Taking a warm bath.
- Reading a book or magazine (choose something light).
- Listening to soft music.
- Doing some easy stretches.
- Listening to a book on tape.
- Having a milky drink (avoid caffeine).

(Smith, Saison and Segal 2010)

129

Whose Responsibility?

Whilst I have highlighted the fact that employers have a responsibility to ensure that staff are not adversely affected by stress, this Pocket Guide has focussed on what social workers themselves can do to respond to stress and avoid burnout in their work.

There are undoubtedly aspects of stress in social work which employers need to look at strategically and there are actions which managers need to take to support social workers and provide an effective working environment. However, social workers themselves do have a responsibility to do what they can to address stress. If as social workers we take a proactive approach, recognising our personal responsibilities to enhance our skills and manage the stress we inevitably face this will go a long way to ensuring we avoid burnout.

How?

Putting it All Together

The 'How' part of this Pocket Guide is significantly bigger than the 'What' and the 'Why' sections. This reflects the fact that the Guide is supposed to be practical to provide some specific ideas and tools to support social workers in responding effectively to the stress they will inevitably face in their work.

I am aware, particularly as a social work practitioner, that you could read this section of the Guide and think "there's nothing new for me here." That may well be the case – but remember, the more stressed we are, the more readily we are able to dismiss potential stress management strategies as 'nothing new' or 'unworkable'.

Take the time to try some of the methods proposed in this Pocket Guide. Be systematic – reflect on which strategies appeal to you the most and try them.

✓ Remember that stress in itself isn't negative. It's your choice how you respond to stress.

✓ Reflect on how you do respond to stress. Think about using a model like a SWOT analysis.

✓ Don't hide any stress you are feeling. Challenge the stigma by talking about how you feel.

✓ Take care of yourself: remember that a healthy balanced lifestyle is one of the best defences against stress and burnout.

✓ Develop positive thinking: try to find a 'mantra' that works for you.

✓ Plan your CPD: take control of your career.

✓ Recognise every achievement: even the small things count.

How?

- ✓ Work on your time management skills.

- ✓ Develop your skills in conflict management.

- ✓ Use reflective practice techniques.

- ✓ Recognise when you feel stressed and do something to help you relax.

- ✓ Develop and use support networks.

- ✓ Make effective use of supervision.

- ✓ Acknowledge that change will always be a part of social work and reflect on how you can best respond.

- ✓ Revisit your 'core': why are you a social worker?

**Most of all take pride in being a social worker.
Every one of us does a vital job.**

References

Alford, L. (2010) *What men should know about the impact of physical activity on their health.* International Journal of Clinical Practice, 64 (13) pp 1731-1734.

ANAS (2010) *Proposition de recommendation IFSW sur le burn out.* Available online at www.ifsw.org/p38002013.html. Accessed 2.11.10.

Bailey, G. (2010) *Innagural Speech as IFSW President to IFSW General Meeting: Hong Kong.*

Borisoff, D. and Victor, D.A. (1998) *Conflict Management: A Communication Skills Approach.* (2nd edition) (Boston) Allyn and Bacon.

Capstick, B. (2010) *Being Positive About Change.* Available online at http://capsticksaxton.com/index/php?option=com-content&view Accessed 1.1.11.

How?

Carver, C., Scheier, M. and Weintraub, J. (1989) *Assessing Coping Strategies: A Theoretically based approach*. Journal of Personality and Social Psychology, 56, pp 267-283.

Collins, S. (2007) *Statutory Social Workers: Stress, Job Satisfaction, Coping, Social Support and Individual Differences*. British Journal of Social Work, 38 (6) pp 1173-1193.

Compassion Fatigue Awareness Project (2010) *What is Compassion Fatigue?* Available online at www.compassionfatigue.org/pages/compassionfatigue.html. Accessed 12.12.10.

Coulshed, V. and Mullender, A. (2006) *Management in Social Work*. (Basingstoke) Palgrave.

Croucher, R. (2010) *Stress and Burnout in Ministry*. Available online at www.churchlink.com.au/churchlink/forum/r_croucher/stress_burnout.html. Accessed 9.12.10.

Dolgoff, R., Loewenberg, F. and Harrington, D. (2008) *Ethical Decisions for Social Work Practice*. (8th edition) (Belmont, Canada) Thomson Brooks / Cole.

Eborall, C. (2003) *Workforce Intelligence Unit Annual Report 2003*. (Leeds) Topss England.

Ellis, A. (1962) *Optimizing Rational Self Talk for Health, Happiness and Wellbeing*. Available online at www.lifeskillstraining.org/cog-restructuring.htm. Accessed 2.3.08.

European Agency for Safety and Health at Work (2010) *Stress*. Available online at http://osha.europa.eu?en/topics/stress/index_html. Accessed 20.12.10.

Figley, C.R. (Ed) (1995) *Compassion Fatigue: Secondary Traumatic Stress Disorders from Treating the Traumatised*. (New York) Brunner.

Friedsocialworker.com (2009) *Preventing Burnout in Human Services*. Available online at www.friedsocialworker.com/Articles/burnoutinhumanservices.htm. Accessed 22.12.10.

Grant, L. and Kinman, G. (2009) *Developing Emotional Resilience in Social Work Students: Supporting Effective Reflective Practitioners.* Presentation at JSWEC Conference 2009.

Health and Safety Executive (2007) *Managing the causes of work related stress: A step by step approach to using the management standards.* (London) HSE.

Health and Safety Executive (2008) *Working Together to Reduce Stress: A Guide for Employees.* (London) HSE.

Health and Safety Executive (2009) *A Guide for employers on making the management standards work.* (London) HSE.

ISMA (2009) *International Stress Management Association UK: Top Ten Stress Busting Tips.* Available online at www.isma.org.uk/about-stress/top-10-stress-busting-tips.html. Accessed 29.12.10.

Jones, C. (2001) *Voices from the frontline: State social workers and new labour.* British Journal of Social Work, 31 (4) pp 547-563.

Jones, R. (2011) *The Glue that Binds*. Professional Social Work. February 2011. pp 18-20

Karasek, R.A. (1979) *Job Demands, job decision latitude and mental strain: Implications for job redesign*. Administrative Science Quarterly, 24 pp 285-308.

Kadushin, A. (1992) *Supervision in social work*. (3rd ed)(New York) Columbia University Press.

Kotter, J.L. (2002) *The Heart of Change: Real Life Stories of How People Change Their Organizations*. (Harvard) Harvard Business Press.

Lazarus, R.S. (1966) *Psychological Stress and the Coping Process*. (New York) McGraw-Hill.

Lazarus, R.S. and Folkman, S. (1984) *Stress, Appraisal and Coping*. (New York) Springer.

Lloyd, C., King, R. and Chenoweth, L. (2002) *Social work stress and burnout: A review*. Journal of Mental Health, 11 (3) pp 255-265.

- A favourite book or magazine
- Some special treats
- Positive images and photographs which bring back positive memories

What would you include in your own stress aid kit?

Teams can also develop something along the lines of stress aid kits – in my team we have a jar of stress biscuits. If one of us goes to take a biscuit from the jar it shows others that they are feeling stressed and promotes some discussion around that – encouraging a supportive team environment.

123

Maslach, C. and Jackson, S.E. (1981) *The measurement of experienced burnout.* Journal of Occupational Behaviour 2 pp 99-113.

Maslach, C. and Leiter, M. (1997) *The Truth about Burnout: How Organisations cause personal stress and what to do about it.* (San Francisco) Jossey Bass.

McGregor, K. (2010) *Just Say No!* Community Care 30.9.10 pp 28-29.

McKenna, C. (2006) *Understanding Secondary Trauma.* Available online at www.buzzle.com/editorials/6-27-2006-100635.asp. Accessed 11.12.10.

McKinnon , K.D. (1998) *Coping with Caring:* The dangers of chronic stress and burnout. Available online at www.charityvillage.com/cv/research/rpersdv1.html. Accessed 30.12.10.

Milczarek, M., Schneider, E. and Gonzalez, E. (2009) *European Risk Observatory Report. OSH in Figures: Stress at Work – Facts and Figures.* (Luxembourg) European Agency for Safety and Health at Work.

Mind Tools (2010) *What Stress Is…..Definitions*. Available online at www.mindtools.com/stress/understandstress/stressdefinition.htm. Accessed 22.12.10.

Morrison, T. (2005) *Staff Supervision in Social Care: Making a Real Difference for Staff and Service Users*. (Brighton) Pavilion Publishing Ltd.

Morrow, A. (2010) *Stress Definition*. Available online at www.dying.about.com/od/glossary/g/stress.htm. Accessed 22.12.10.

Pfifferling, J.H. and Gilley, K. (2000) *Overcoming Compassion Fatigue*. Family Practice Management. Available online at www.aafp.org/fpm/20000400/39over.html. Accessed 20.12.10.

Porter, L., Bingley, G. and Steers, R. (1982) *Motivation and Work Behaviour*. (New York) Mc Graw-Hill.

Rose, M. (2003) *Good Deal? Bad Deal? Job Satisfaction in Occupations*. Work Employment and Society, 17 (3) pp 503-530.

Rushton, A. (1987) *Stress among social workers*. In Payne, R., Firth-Cozens, J. (Eds) Stress in Health Professionals. (Chichester) John Wiley.

Schiraldi, G.R. (2009) *The Post-Traumatic Stress Disorder Source Book: A Guide to Healing, Recovery and Growth*. (New York) McGraw Hill.

Segal, J. (2008) *The Language of Emotional Intelligence*. (London) McGraw Hill.

Segal, S. and Smith, M. (2010) *Conflict Resolution Skills: Building the Skills that can turn conflicts into opportunities*. Available online at http://helpguide.org/mental/eq8_conflict_resolution.htm. Accessed 10.2.11

Selye, H. (1975) *Confusion and Controversy in the Stress Field*. Journal of Human Stress, 1 pp 37-44.

Smith, M., Jaffe-Gill, E., Segal, J. and Segal, R. (2010) *Preventing Burnout: Signs, Symptoms and Coping Strategies*. Available online at www.helpguide.org/mental/burnout_signs_symptoms.htm. Accessed 28.12.10.

Smith, M., Saison, J. and Segal, R. (2010) *How to Sleep Better: Tips for Getting a Good Night's Sleep*. Available online at http://helpguide.org/life/sleep_tips.htm. Accessed 22.12.10.

Stamm, B. (2009) *Advances in the Theory of Compassion Satisfaction and Fatigue and its measurement with the ProQol 5*. (Atlanta) International Society for Traumatic Stress Studies.

Swinton, L. (2010) *The 7 Best Stress Management Techniques I Know*. Available online at www.mftrou.com/stress-management-techniques.html. Accessed 12.1.11.

Taylor, S. (2006) *A Clinician's Guide to Post Traumatic Stress Disorder: A Cognitive Behavioural Approach*. (New York) Guildford Press.

Thomas, K. W. and Kilmann, R. H. (1974) *Thomas-Kilmann Conflict Mode Instrument*. (California) Xicom.

Wilkinson, G. (2003) *Understanding Stress*. (London) British Medical Association.